Conquer bad attitude:

Way to Figure Out How Your Life Will Change If Your Attitude Changes.

Muhammed Ashraph

Table of contents

Chapter one

Meaning of Attitude

Social psychologists scarcely demonstrate any unanimity in establishing a definition of attitude. Some behaviouristically minded social psychologists refer to attitudes as conforming behavior. The conduct is geared towards a certain standard or norm.

One cannot talk about uniformity if there is no standard or norm. Attitudes are created concerning events, individuals, or groups with whom someone comes in touch in course of the growth and development of his personality.

Attitude is a functional state of preparedness that directs the organism to respond in a specific manner to particular stimuli or sensory conditions.

According to Murphy & Murphy, attitude is a means of being set towards or against specific things. Baldwin argues that attitude is preparedness for attention or action of a certain pattern. In the perspective of Warren, the precise mental disposition toward an incoming experience whereby the experience is transformed or state of preparedness for a given sort of action is referred to as attitude.

Cantril thinks that an attitude is a more or less permanently persistent state of readiness of mental organization which predisposes a person to respond distinctively to any object or circumstance with which it is associated.

Attitude may alternatively be described as a mental or neurological state of readiness structured by experience impacting dynamically or directly the individuals' behavior to all things and events with which it is associated.

Some others have claimed that attitude is a learned or more or less structured propensity to behave persistently generally negatively or favorably with relation to some circumstance, concept, object, or class of such items.

Attitudes govern the organism's direction towards its social and physical surroundings including oneself. Because of a certain attitude towards specific stimuli, impulses are awakened and action is mobilized to approach or avoid the stimulus.

Kretch and Crutchfield and Ballachey think that attitudes have an adoptive relevance in that they reflect a basic psychological connection between a person's capacity to detect feel and learn while offering order and meaning to his continual experience in a complicated social context.

Rosnow and Robinson argue that the word attitude implies the organization in a person of his emotions, beliefs, and predispositions to act as he does. Fishbein and Ajzen (1975) have sought to emphasize the evaluative component when attempting to define attitude.

Attitude is a taught inclination to react in a consistently positive or negative way about a certain object. This concept, then, highlights the notion that attitudes are primarily judgments of a specific person, group, their behaviors and objects, circumstances, etc.

Some have also sought to characterize attitudes based on their components or structures. Such components include the cognitive component, emotive component, and behavioral component.

(a) The cognitive component of a social attitude consists of a person's system of beliefs, perceptions, and preconceptions about the attitudinal object. In other words, it relates to his beliefs on the item. The word opinion is sometimes used as a replacement for the cognitive component of an attitude especially when it is related to some topic or problem.

(b) The affective component of a social attitude refers to the emotional part of the attitude which is very frequently a deep established component that resists most change. In other words, it reveals the direction and intensity of an individual's appraisal.

In additional basic words, it includes a form of emotion experienced towards the object of attitude say love or hate, like or dislike, pleasant or disagreeable sentiments. The emotional component as previously said is pretty powerful and generally stands in the path of attitude transformation.

(c) Finally, the behavioral component of social attitudes reveals the inclination to behave towards the object of attitude in particular specified ways. In other words, it is a tendency to behave in a specific way towards the attitude object. This is known through monitoring the conduct of the person i.e., what he claims he will do or really how he behaves, does, or responds.

A person who shows a strong unpalatable attitude towards dowry by not accepting any dowry during his marriage or a person who fights against corruption by remaining honest and upright throughout his life and by not allowing and tolerating injustice to occur with his knowledge is an example demonstrating the behavioral component of attitude.

Results reveal that there is an internal structure among these components of the attitude. Thus, certain attitudes build interlinks with other attitudes to produce structured patterns instead of existing in isolation from one another.

From this, it can be argued that the above three components of attitude are connected and a change in one component is likely to generate a change in others to preserve internal consistency within the entire attitude structure.

Further, these components may either stay at a basic level or a complicated level depending upon their power. For instance, if the emotional component is at a basic level, it may include plain liking or dislike for the attitudinal object whereas a sophisticated affective component may cause feelings of love or hate, rage or contempt, fear, anxiety, etc.

In the same manner, the cognitive component at a basic level may have adequate information about the attitudinal object while at a complex level, he has a thorough system of beliefs and clear concepts about the attitudinal object in the issue.

The conduct component normally relies upon the cognitive and emotional components as they ordinarily guide his behavior maintaining other elements constant since other aspects than attitude also control one's behavior.

Though normally consistency exists between the emotional and cognitive components, the link between them and the conduct component frequently appears to be inconsistent holds.

Mann also argues that the complexity and strength of the individual components have major consequences for the creation and effective adjustments of an attitude.

He is of opinion that attitude with poor cognitive component i.e., having little understanding about the item is likely to be exceedingly unstable and transient. During childhood, while attitudes are in the formative stage, all three components play crucial roles.

But eventually, the individual grows more selective and so, the cognitive component becomes more significant. The aforesaid three components including the cognitive component, emotional component, and behavioral component comprise the structure of attitude.

Based on the above facts and definitions or the 'what' of attitude, attitude can be broadly defined as a relatively permanent system of the organization of the behavior shown by an individual towards an object, person, event, action, or stimulus and this stable mental organization ordinarily have cognitive, affective and action or behavior components which interact with each other and influence an individuals behavior in different ways.

Chapter Two

CONCEPT OF ATTITUDE

The idea of attitude is possibly the most important and unique term in current social psychology. The study of the idea of attitude is significant for psychologists and notably social psychologists and sociologists.

As a result of contact between the person and the community certain views, attitudes, values, norms, practices, and traditions arise with which the individual typically complies. Through the process of socialization, the human being adheres to these societal standards and traditional beliefs. Socialization develops mostly via attitude and confirming behaviors.

This confirmation of social traditions, customs, and cultural values happen via the establishment of acceptable and positive thoughts and ideas in connection to different socially standardized values, norms, rules, regulations, or various other standards of behavior of his reference groups. This is alternatively termed attitude in a larger sense. The sociogenic and biogenic reasons of a person are also reflected in his views.

From the aforesaid standpoint, the attitude has got broad-reaching ramifications in one's social, personal, and emotional life. It not only affects the behavior of an individual in a certain circumstance, but it also leads the person to behave in a particular situation, it also tells the person to act in a particular way by offering a prepared set.

Thus, G.W. Allport accurately remarks, "The idea of attitude is undoubtedly the most unique and essential term in current social psychology." After a lengthy interval of roughly sixty years probably the veracity of the preceding assertion remains.

Still, lots of investigations are being undertaken in the domain of attitude and social distance which reveal its relevance in the social life of human beings.

Murphy and New Comb have also stressed the aforesaid aspects. They argue that possibly no one notion within the entire area of social psychology has a more nearly pivotal position than that of attitudes.

Characteristics and Properties of Attitudes

1. Attitudes always entail a subject-object interaction. They are related to ideas, methods, and exterior things. It is usually tied to distinct stimuli circumstances.

This stimulation scenario may be towards:

(a) Objects such as a house, vehicle, TV, kitchen

(b) Persons like own self, father, mother, in-laws, brother, sister, etc.

(c) Institutions like school, college, church, club

(d) Concepts, values, norms, and symbols like the flag, truth, democracy, justice, religion, God, philosophy, etc. These subject object connections are not inherent nor biologically determined but learned from the environment. An individual's attitude, therefore, arranges his actions regarding a certain object.

2. Attitudes in connection to things, individuals and values may or may not have motivational appeal initially. Gradually people via social connection acquire either a good or negative attitude that relies upon their experience and needs.

In other words, the person first comes in touch with some items and develops a certain liking or dislikeness based upon the satisfaction of his desire or motivation or owing to any other causes.

The organism first senses and then forms an attitude. Thus, the perceptual stage is most crucial especially if there is no incentive. Many social attitudes are discovered to form via verbal evaluations of adults even if there may not be any reason.

3. Attitudes offer a direction to one's behaviors and activities. Because of a certain good attitude the organism either approaches it or because of a negative attitude avoids it. A positive attitude will encourage the conduct and aid in its persistence. A negative attitude opposite will make the reaction weak and eventually lead to avoidance conduct.

4. Attitudes are colored with motivational and evaluative features. A good attitude is seen as having some beneficial qualities

whereas a bad attitude is looked at as having disagreeable and undesirable consequences. The directive characteristics or attitude make our objective purposeful and guide our conduct.

5. Attitudes are not natural but learned, acquired, and conditioned. They develop in the community in the brains of men via different kinds of instruction. As a consequence of our first-hand and second-hand experience with things, thoughts, and situations and via the process of social contact and socialization attitudes evolve.

Direct or direct experience is likely the essential ingredient in the creation and evolution of attitudes. But frequently the attitude of our parents, family, friends, teachers, classmates, and course loved ones, and attitude of the society aids in the formation of an individual's attitude in a specific direction. Thus, the attitude develops both via direct and indirect factors.

6. Attitude is never neutral. It can be either positive or negative, favorable or unfavorable, palatable or unpalatable. Thus, it is always tinted with some type of emotion. A neutral perspective is defined to be the viewpoint and not attitude when there is no emotional tone.

7. Attitudes have emotional characteristics of varying degrees. They are related to sentiments and emotions like pleasant, unpleasant, fear, and love. An attitude that functions as a predisposition for future action is characterized by emotionality. The response is either moderate or strong or normal. The emotional feeling tone in attitude may be related to motivation as stated previously.

The person is obliged to acquire either a positive or an unfavorable attitude because of the pressure of the social environment or owing to the nature of the response of one individual to another individual which is constantly associated with some emotional tone.

8. Attitudes are more or less lasting organizations or enduring states of preparedness. Thus, sentiments once acquired and largely steady, consistent, and permanent may be typically expected. The cognitive component growing during the perceptual stage renders attitude relatively persistent. If you have enjoyed a specific genre of music like light music, you would tend to appreciate it at least for quite a long duration.

But it does not imply that attitudes are absolute and permanent phases of preparedness or are inflexible, and consequently not susceptible to change. The simple fact that attitudes are learned behavior suggests that they may be modified by further learning or experience. It may be enhanced or lessened, can be transformed from tasty to disagreeable or from favorable to unfavorable and vice versa.

9. From the aforementioned facts, it follows that attitudes may be modified based upon the circumstances, experiences, and how of information via different modes of communication or through direct engagement. A lot of research on attitude transformation corroborates the aforementioned truth.

10. Attitude is termed the evaluative attitude towards the social environment which is primarily expressed verbally and, thus, may be quantified. In attitude, the degree of emotion is assessed using a five-point or six-point scale like very favorable, favorable, moderately favorable, neither favorable nor unfavorable, unfavorable, and highly unfavorable.

You may show your stance towards the radicals generating difficulties in Kashmir or Assam via the above scale, by expressing very much against them, moderately against them, or firmly in support of them, etc.

11. Attitudes comprise cognitive, emotional, and behavioral components.

12. Attitudes vary in the amount and diversity of stimuli to which they are related. The strength and range of an attitude rely upon the strength of the experience and learning of the organism.

If the organism has been taught that individuals of a specific caste are inferior, he would have a negative attitude toward such castes. Similarly, if anyone is taught from the youth that ladies are psychologically weaker than boys he would acquire the same attitude towards girls in general until otherwise occurs.

13. Except for a handful, most of the attitudes are grouped or connected. If you have a bad attitude towards the male sex, every other thing, concept, value, or occurrence relating to men people, in general, will likewise be looked upon similarly.

Thus, attitudes typically get ordered and organized when associated substantially with other attitudes. Only a handful few attitudes can be conceived as living in isolation. Strong attitudes constitute the heart of a cluster of attitudes. Around these attitudes which stay at the center, other connected attitudes are grouped.

Classification of Attitude

Attitudes have been characterized in numerous ways such as positive and negative, common or personal, reciprocal, etc.

Based on the current link between the person the society many sorts of attitudes develop:

(a) Reciprocal attitude: The attitude between the employee and the employer, student, and instructor is reciprocal. Such attitudes are categorized as reciprocal ones.

(b) Common attitude: When a huge number of people in the community have a similar or uniform attitude towards an organization, groups or political parties, religion, etc. it is known as a common attitude. If the majority of the individuals in a specific community do not want to receive a dowry, this is viewed as a common attitude.

(c) Private attitude: The term itself is informative. Such sentiments are the individual's unique attitudes and are not shared by others. Likeness or dislikeness for a certain individual falls under this category.

But fully private sentiments are seldom seen.

Sometimes individuals acquire hidden goals which are not reciprocal nor shared but private. Most persons have hidden regions of guilt and they frequently take intricate measures to disguise their guilt sentiments from others.

Attitudes also create a hierarchical order. Every individual assigns more emphasis to certain attitudes and less to others. Attitude is also selective. The selected character of the attitude is a result of the variables inside the person himself. This suggests a functional state of preparedness regarding the stimuli in the issue. The psychology of attitude is closely tied to the general selectivity of the entire organism.

Attitudes may also be categorized in the following fashion into six groups:

I Theoretical (ii) Economic (iii) (iii) Aesthetic (iv) Social (v) Political (vi) Religious.

(I) Theoretical: Those who constantly strive to uncover the causes and truth behind everything belong under this group. Hearing a wonderful narrative, a mathematician asked “Beautiful, but what does it prove?” Scientists, philosophers, and academics are of this sort. Their outlook is more conceptually oriented.

(ii) Economic: Guided by the utility and practical value of an item economic-type folks strive to figure out the benefit and usefulness of a thing. Their approach towards anything is utility orientated. They are extremely practical individuals. They appraise individuals based on their earning ability. If there is a flood, they will be keen to hear how it has economically impacted the flood-ravaged communities.

(iii) Aesthetic: People holding aesthetic views strive to uncover the beauty of a thing. It assists in satisfaction and self-development. They like to envision lovely things and get joy out of them. If there is a flood they travel by the lovely landscape or unpleasant sights.

(iv) Social: Persons with social attitudes assess the situation from the social aspect. It entails love for fellowmen and self-sacrifice. It is possibly the most respectful attitude in life. Such folks endeavor to aid those in trouble. Gopabandhu Das was a person with a social mindset.

(v) Political: People with a political mindset seek to dominate and control other people. They are lovers of power. They strive to manage a situation via self-exhibition. Such individuals desire to be leaders and rise over others for the sake of power. Politicians fall within this area.

(vi) Religious: The urge to study the last mystery of nature, the mystic element of existence is prevalent among those with a religious mindset. Such attitude is characterized by religion and belief and emotion and is not influenced by thinking.

Individuals of all other attitudes would attempt to study the cause of the flood with a reason but people with religious attitudes would argue that God's wish has been executed and that what God has done is for the well-being of the people. They will never blame God for anything whatsoever, rather they may state that because of heaps of corruption, God has grown furious with humanity and chastised them in this manner.

Functions of Attitude

A person, throughout his lifetime, is obliged to adopt certain attitudes. These sentiments may be positive or adverse or both. The personality of a person is influenced by his attitude. Attitudes shape one's personality.

A person might be termed good or bad, social or unsociable, acceptable or objectionable depending upon his attitude. If a person generally develops a bad attitude, his life becomes terrible. He cannot accept or believe or love anyone. He becomes social or antisocial. Conversely, nobody will welcome him since this is a reciprocal process.

From the above standpoints, it is perfectly obvious that attitude influences one's conduct, one's personality, and one's status in society. While a good attitude towards others makes him nice, friendly, and attractive, negative attitudes produce many adversaries and build hostile sentiments and hate in his head.

Attitudes have, therefore, crucial roles in shaping, influencing, and deciding one's conduct in all settings. As previously established, based on attitude personality may be typed.

Attitudes operate as a source of motivation which aids in the adjustment to the environment. According to Katz (1960), four major personality roles are fulfilled by the maintenance and adjustments of social attitudes. They are adjustment, value expression, knowledge, and ego defense.

I Adjustment Function:\sThe holding of a given attitude leads to reward or the avoidance of punishment. It is the utilitarian or instrumental function of attitude which pushes the individual to adapt to the surroundings to achieve social acceptance and support from family, friends, and neighbors.

In the case of some social concerns like marriage, death, democracy, religion, sacrifice, and helping others, he has ideas similar to his parents and relatives, and friends. Further pleasant attitudes are created towards those stimuli which meet one’s wants and unfavorable attitudes towards those which stand for the satisfaction of his needs and motivations.

(ii) Value Expression Function:\sOn the basis of identification with parents and other relatives the kid develops specific personal values and self notions. These ideals are interwoven in the shape of diverse attitudes. Attitudes aid in conveying these ideals. The individual obtains pleasure via expressing views according to his particular ideals.

Religious, ideological, and patriotic views and ideals generally are founded on this function. People obtain personal pleasure by involving themselves in social work, caring for old individuals, assisting at the time of floods and famines, taking care of orphans, or raising their voices against corruption and social injustice.

(iii) Knowledge Function:\sAccording to Mann this function of attitude is founded on the urge to comprehend, make meaning and offer proper structure to the world. Attitudes have a cognitive function in the sense that they aid in comprehending things correctly for the goal of speedy adjustment.

Attitudes that are insufficient in coping with new and changing conditions are abandoned since, otherwise, they lead to inconsistencies and inconsistency. The demand for cognitive consistency, meaning, and clarity is met by the knowledge function of attitude.

(iv) Ego Defense Function:\sThe ego defensive function of attitude gives protection against the understanding and acceptance of fundamental painful facts concerning sickness, death, weakness, instability, frustration, unemployment, illness, and several other harsh realities of life.

By rationalizing and distorting views on the aforementioned harsh facts of life the ego seeks to protect itself and lead a happy existence by avoiding unhappiness resulting from these painful truths. All these facts lead us to think about the huge relevance of the functions of attitude in human existence.

chapter Three

FORMATION OF ATTITUDE

Attitudes are not biologically inherited but created out of constant encounters with the world around us. They are the product of a complicated function of both cultural and functional variables. From birth onwards, every person is subjected to direct and indirect stimuli of the environment which educate him to hold specific ideas, values, and views.

Through the process of socialization when one is taught to correlate pleasant or terrible sensations, dos or do not, positive and unfavorable experiences with specific acts or behavioral patterns, he acquires certain consistent attitudes. When certain actions are rewarded one develops a pleasant attitude towards them and any action or opinion which is penalized one develops an undesirable attitude towards it.

Attitudes can arise when one imitates his parents and other personal acquaintances, and connections. Children and adults establish views very frequently based on recommendations and second-hand experiences. Many individuals are also observed adopting views spontaneously based on their own personal and first-hand experiences. Nevertheless, attitudes evolve in the mind of someone via the process of socialization.

Social attitudes grow out of verbal value assessments, dos, and do Not. But personal attitudes may evolve out of one's interaction, contact, and direct experience with the attitudinal objects and other objects associated with it. In the case of social attitudes, one is trained to adopt a specific attitude towards an attitudinal object like "Mama says not to play with girls" or blacks.

Parents, family members, media and press, classmates, instructors, and well-wishers acquaintances, all have a huge part in the creation and evolution of views. Some research about attitudes and values of American, British, and Indian pupils and Indian and Western Children is extremely interesting.

Through attitudinal socialization experiences, individuals begin to acquire proper attitudes towards particular persons, various sorts of food, toy, playmates, and play materials and develop bad attitudes against others. According to Sherif, our attitudes are concentrated on the objects of values which may be social institutions, persons, neutral items, parties, etc.

The formation of values out of which attitudes are created is the product of social traditions, customs learning, and social institutions. Initially, the newborn being solely concerned with satisfying his fundamental requirements like feeding and care is socially blind and is not bothered about the social punishments.

Through the process of need fulfillment, the youngster receives a scope to develop an attitude. Those items and individuals who meet his requirements he develops a pleasant attitude towards them. But when an item or person stands in the path of his desire fulfillment, an adverse attitude develops towards it.

In his usual conduct, he never reveals the developed direction of attitude. So until the preschool age i.e., the third or fourth year, attitude in its genuine sense does not exist.

But when the youngster gets to school, certain values and practices are placed upon him and these values eventually become the core of attitude development. In the beginning, the child's mental level is less grown, his values are shapeless and the attitude development is in a fully defused stage. Piaget and others have believed that the kid in his disposition to a dog, football player, or an actress never exhibits the different tinges of attitude which are the features of an adult.

To all these items, he would just declare like or detest but he cannot differentiate. At this stage, there is no selectivity of perception which is essential for the establishment of attitude. This selectivity of vision and values eventually develop in children out of which attitudes are created.

This is termed differentiation to the items or stimuli around him which increases over years. In the beginning, the child reacts equally say to three different objects. But as the distinction is built up, he becomes empathetic and protective of the dog or demands from his mother or respects an actor.

These obvious cut differentiations throughout the years suggest that attitude undergoes growth in a social setting relying upon its existing cultural pattern and social penalties. After differentiation integration of multiple value systems and attitudes which embrace them take place.

This offers a direction to any attitude. For this, cognitive clarity is crucial. Depending upon the value ascribed to a given attitudinal object, positive or negative attitudes arise. As the kid achieves maturity via authority, status, recognition, social acceptance, incentives, and punishment, he increasingly attends to the social world.

In essence, plenty of attitudes emerge out of fulfillment or dissatisfaction with demands. Attitude towards Jews, Blacks, and Whites, socio-economically backward groups, items, and individuals arise out of this. The hatred of the ingroup against the outgroup is shown in his behaviors vocal or nonverbal and strongly associated with the dissatisfaction with their wants.

Secondly, many of our attitudes also evolve owing to the second level and indirect experience like TV, radio, and newspapers to which the person is exposed every day. These mass communication media truly are accountable for the formation of many of our attitudes in the present day.

The cognitive components of the attitude largely grow out of this indirect and second-hand information, the communication channels. The views may be correct or wrong, but clearly, the communication network plays a significant part in the creation of attitudes.

One's membership in the organization aids in the building of attitude. He typically embraces the views created by such groups, maybe his family school, neighborhood, peer groups, different connections, and social and ethnic groupings. However, there may be some exceptions and individual variances depending upon the nature of the concerned individual. Personality plays a significant part contributing in to the variety of attitudes.

The function of main groups such as family, friends, coworkers, etc. contribute to the creation of attitude, studies by Campbell, Gurin, and Miller corroborate the above position. Similarity and attractiveness also aid in the development of attitudes.

The attitudes which start developing continually from infancy may have been transformed by the time, we are adults but the process of acquisition and development of attitudes continues.

According to learning and reinforcement theorists, attitudes are taught behavior to certain stimuli. These theorists have focussed on determining the nature of the cues that drive one to form and sustain particular attitudes.

Staats (1975), and Staas and Staas (1958) have sought to explain the creation of attitudes via fundamental learning processes. After coupling a U.S. such as meat with a C.S. such as a bell Pavlov observed that just ringing the bell started to induce a new reaction i.e., saliva.

According to Staats, an attitude is the counterpart of a C.R., something that may be evoked by the introduction of a C.S. The findings of Staats's research done to illustrate that attitudes may be classically conditioned, suggested simply that individuals had more favorable sentiments towards the nations connected with positive terms and more negative attitudes towards those linked with negative phrases.

Of course, the preceding research of Staats has been questioned on various grounds by

Page (1969). (1969). But new evidence does reveal that folks linked with dangerous conditions tend to take on undesirable attributes merely by association. This directly confirms the classical conditioning theory of attitude development proposed by Staats.

Our daily experiences also highlight the role of classical conditioning in the establishment of attitude. Through this strategy, it is discovered, that individuals demonstrate intense attitudinal responses to social items even in the absence of first-hand direct experience.

It is because of this that when children overhear repeated pairings of words in the conversation of their parents throughout the early years of life, (like Reema—naughty, San—very handsome) form negative or positive attitudes themselves even if they have never come in direct contact with the attitudinal stimulus itself.

Chapter Four

CONCEPT OF BEHAVIOR P

Consequently, the topic requires an extremely explicit explanation for greater comprehension.

What then is behavior? “Behaviour may be described as any activity or action of a living body displayed either consciously or subconsciously which can be noticed either directly or indirectly by another person.”
In this situation, behavior may vary from such basic tasks as sleeping, and playing with a friend, to such complicated ones as obtaining a new skill, teaching young children, managing a major company, and leading a multi-ethnic/religious nation like the USA, UK, or Poland.

Behavior may also be good or negative, normal or aberrant, inborn or acquired, internal or external. All these sorts of activities are under the scope of psychology.

Types And Aspects Of Behaviour

The effort to divide behaviors into several kinds is solely for intellectual or academic convenience. Otherwise, the two categories of behavior typically identified by psychologists (i.e overt and covert behaviors), are interrelated since the former is nothing but an open representation of the latter. However, besides the two categories as typically described by psychologists, behaviors may also be characterized based on the processes by which they emerge and the reasons which they seek to meet or the settings under which they are expressed.

These characteristics of conduct may be displayed openly or covertly and may be used to evaluate the person.

For our purpose thus, conduct may be categorized as follows:

1. Overt Behaviour
This covers all such activities or acts of a living entity, which may be witnessed immediately by another person when such actions are exhibited. Activities such as walking, jogging, laughing, weeping, eating, cooking, reading, etc., are instances of overt conduct. Our perception of people and our interactions with them are mostly dependent on their overt conduct.

2. Overt Behaviour
This element of behavior involves such internal physiological processes and activities of a person that cannot be seen openly or noticed immediately by only looking, except by the use of specific tools or procedures. Examples of such behaviors are thinking, sleeping, heartbeat, variations in pulse rate and blood pressure, processes of digestion, sense of hunger, etc.

3. Genetically Inherited Behaviour

This encompasses all such behaviors that are conveyed from parents to their offspring via genetic processes and such behavioral features that are specific to persons of the same biological origin. They also include such behavior that is exclusive to certain kinds of animals.

For instance, some conduct features are exclusive to people of the same parentage or biological origin. This may be found in this pronunciation of words, either in English or French, regardless withstanding the educational background or social orientation of such persons.

Even such other behavioral characteristics as stammering, thieving, over-anxiousness, cleverness, etc., may be genetically conveyed from parents to their direct off-spring or second or third-generation offspring. Is there any wonder then that in some parts of Nigeria, particularly, Igbo land, before marriage is finally contracted, the families of the couple concerned will make inquiries to find out how the parents of the would-be couple had lived or whether there is any case of mental problem or criminal tendencies that can be traced to the parents of either of the couple.

Again again, the barking behavior of dogs is a genetically passed characteristic. The new dog begins barking without needing to learn it. Therefore, such conduct is species-specific. And it is also specific to animals belonging to the dog family. There is also a larger probability of persons either whose parents a twins giving birth to twins.

4. Socially Acquired Behaviour

There are such behaviors that are learned either consciously or unconsciously dealing with persons of diverse socio-cultural groups and backgrounds. This also covers such behavior established via the process of formal learning and socialization. For instance, we improve language proficiency through engaging with or learning from others that use the same language. Besides, our method of clothing, choice of food and the way we consume, and even some undesired habits, are adopted when we engage and mingle with other people.

Behaviour May Also Be Classified As Formal Or Informal

1. It is considered to be formal when such conduct pattern follows specific written down standards aimed at reaching a certain purpose or aims. For instance, our behavior in learning or working contexts is generally formal.

2. On the other hand, informal behavior includes the ones displayed while we engage with people or communicate with our social surroundings informally. In reality, conduct may be regarded to be informed when it does not follow any written out standards or

principles. For example, street fighting, joking with playmates, etc., occur under informal conduct.
Besides, conduct may be either normal or deviant, based on its conformity with, or divergence from the cultural norms and standards of the community.

Difference between attitude and behavior

Each individual is unique from one another, not just in our physical qualities but mainly so in our actions and attitudes.

'Behavior' is an intrinsic attribute of a creature, including man, towards its surroundings and other species. It is governed by our endocrine and neurological systems and the intricacy of our behavioral patterns is established by the complexity of our neural system.

Our habits are either natural or acquired and taught from our surroundings. It is our reaction to the varied stimuli and other internal or external impulses whether deliberate or not.

‘Attitude’ is how we respond to various events or information. We either have a favorable or negative response towards an item, a person, location, thing, or event. It is how we assess these things and the manner that they affect us that shapes our conduct towards them. We form our attitudes via experience and observation.

Views fluctuate according to our experiences yet inherited factors may also alter our attitudes. Our views may be impacted by several factors:

Intelligence:

Intelligent individuals digest information more completely and are less swayed by one-sided input.

Self-esteem:

People with average self-esteem are more readily persuaded than those with a higher or considerably lower self-esteem.

Credibility:

The reliability of the source of the information, its competence regarding the issue, and general trustworthiness might alter our attitude towards the input.

Presentation:

How the information is presented is highly crucial in the creation of our attitude towards it.

We may also have conscious and unconscious attitudes, rational, or illogical attitudes that incorporate our ideas, emotions, and intuition. Extroversion and introversion are two forms of attitude.

Extroversion is an attitude that is easygoing and confident. People with this mentality draw their drive from other people and prefer to act first before considering it. Introversion is an attitude that is less reliant on external motivation. Introverts frequently ponder before they act and are quiet, subtle, and prefer to work alone.

'Behavior' on the other hand might be common, acceptable, or undesirable. We determine behavior's acceptability by our social standards, and we naturally adhere to these rules. It is regarded as a fundamental human activity, and our conduct is based upon the behavior of others.

These things may alter our behavior:

Genetics. Biological variables may alter the way we react towards specific things.

Attitude. How we respond to situations may alter our conduct.

Social norms. Whether we react to given conduct or not relies on our beliefs.

Control. Our opinion on the ease or complexity of a specific scenario impacts our conduct.

Core faith. This includes encouragement from our family, peers, the media, and society.

Summary:

1. 'Behavior' is an intrinsic property of an organism whereas 'attitude' is a human attribute.
2. Our behavior is governed by our endocrine system but our attitude may be altered by things that might be internal or external.
3. Our actions are established by our societal standards while our attitudes are formed by how we view things.

4. Organisms may have similar behavioral patterns whereas people have attitudes that are separate and different from each other.

Chapter Five

WHAT LEADS TO NEGATIVE ATTITUDE?

Some causes for adopting a pessimistic outlook might be linked to the unpredictability of life. These include sickness and disease, prior trauma, mental health predispositions to sadness or anxiety, and being unusually sensitive to the emotions and experiences of others.

Even while we recognize that a negative and fault-finding viewpoint may impair our physical and mental health, relationships, job performance, and pleasure in life, it might feel hard at times to overcome a poor attitude. To aggravate the situation, we may then chastise ourselves for failing to bring it together. All this might add up to a feeling of despondency.

It may assist to take an honest and sympathetic look at probable reasons why were having such a hard time changing into a more optimistic frame of mind. Once we have a greater knowledge of the origins of our negativity and anxiety, were in a better position to take measures to improve ourselves or receive the outside support we need:

1:We don't want to be disappointed. Daring to hope for the best seems too vulnerable to us. We feel intimidated, like a cornered animal. We've been disappointed by individuals or events in the past and therefore "protect" ourselves by anticipating the worse. We assume that if we don't anticipate anything wonderful to happen, we won't suffer any disappointment when things don't go well. We haven't acquired adequate abilities to cope with things not going our way, so we knock down each relationship or endeavor ahead of time.

2: We've had role models (maybe our parents) with unfavorable views. We've taken up their attitude towards life and made it our habit as well, rather than concentrating on purposefully establishing our own, proactive, and resilient, viewpoint.

3: We don't want to be rejected. If we think that other people may not approve of us, we decide (either consciously or subconsciously) to beat them to the punch and "not like them first". After all, if we minimize someone else's significance or likability, this could lessen any disparaging statement they might make about it - or so we argue. We may also utilize similar thinking when it comes to ourselves. For example, we may remark something self-deprecating like, "I look so obese in this dress" or "I'm such a klutz" before someone else does.

4: We think in black and white terms. If we can't do something flawlessly, we're hesitant to attempt doing it at all. If we can't satisfy everyone, we don't see the sense of being acceptable to anybody at all. This is self-defeating and may cause us to give up on doing anything, even trying to alter our attitude for the better, in the notion that if we lapse and have one negative thought, we have blown it.

5: We create unreasonable expectations or attempt to change too much at one time. Then, when we hit an impediment, we overreact and maybe give up on our goal, which promotes a negative mindset.

6: We assume that any unpleasant sensation is unnecessary and a show of weakness on our behalf. Thus, we give up on ourselves. We fail to recognize (or to believe) that a broad range of emotions is good – the key is in the ratio of the elements. If we were cooking a cake, for instance, the recipe would probably ask for a teaspoon or two of salt. If we put in half a cup of salt, it would be excessive and would destroy the dish. However, we do need the salt — in moderation. Same thing with emotions. It would be absurd to aspire to never, ever become furious, even for one second. What's most important is the prism through which we perceive ourselves, other people, and the world, for the most part.

7: We imagine that fear or fury will invigorate and inspire us to change. While such feelings may kick-start an adrenalin surge and maybe frantic activity in the short run, over the long term they can wear us down, damage our immune system, and lead to despair and anxiety

8: We desire comfort, attention, or aid, however, don't feel capable of asking for these things directly. So, by our indirect words or acts, we attempt to elicit aid from others.

9: We are especially sensitive to mental and/or bodily distress. Some of us are simply more sensitive than others and have a lower pain threshold. This may add to the negativity.

10: We wish to express our uniqueness. We don't want to merely go along with the crowd, therefore we tend to naturally swim against the tide. We fail to recognize that this reaction is just as reactive as simply agreeing with everything.

11: Were unconsciously rehearsing a situation with an authoritative person or someone who dominated us a condition called repetition compulsion. We are attempting to figure out an alternative ending that rules in our favor.

12: We’re used to being the victim rather than an agent of change. We believe that finger-pointing absolves us of the obligation of taking action and altering what we can.

We forget that “that was then, this is now”, and that we may now have more tools at our disposal than we had earlier in our lives.
13: We want to be in control. In a sense, deciding ahead of time that things will not work out provides us with a feeling of predictability.
14: Were HALT – hungry, angry, lonely, or exhausted? Any one of them (and particularly a combination of these variables) may feed irritation, impatience, and depression.

Types of Negative Attitude:

There are some sorts of persons who engage in negative states of mind. They are all distinct in various ways of thinking and behaving, but the uniting element of all of them is their relentless negativity.

Here are numerous sorts of such personalities:

1. Miserable Type.
2. Silent Killer.
3. Drama Queen.
4. Paranoid Type.

1. Miserable Type:

Such folks are irritable from the start of the day. They meet with failures as soon as they get up, which sets their day to be full of wrath and misery. Usually, this sort of individual stays to themselves, and their presence makes others grumpy.

People quickly sense their terrible energy and attempt to keep away from them. The most fascinating feature of this kind is that they are usually ignorant of their mental condition. They don't recognize that they are negative.

2. Silent killer:

Such folks frequently grasp psychology fairly well. They utilize this information to gradually develop hostility, rage, and poor self-esteem in others. They do this by making observations about how others act or appear. They know that their statements are detrimental, but others may not recognize them.

3. Drama Queen:

This is the most prevalent kind. Their emotions span from wrath to self-pity and any tiny event may be converted into a storm. They appear to relish the notion that they can affect how others feel and be the focus of attention.

Such individuals are needy and insecure, they need continual reinforcement. They seek attention and acceptance. If they don't obtain what they want, they begin behaving in juvenile ways. They may start weeping, tossing things around, or attempting to get on others' nerves.

4. Paranoid Type:

They view people to be continually seeking to degrade their life. If they go shopping, they assume that shops are attempting to rip them off. If someone tries to befriend them, they assume that he/she wants something in exchange for the friendship.

Consequences of Negative Attitude:

A bad attitude may bring a lot of trouble for the folks with a negative attitude. It may also bring trouble to the family members and also the others who are around the person with the negative attitude.

Some of the repercussions of a negative attitude are:

1. It shortens life.
2. It generates an uncomfortable future.
3. It damages others.
4. It generates unfavorable consequences.

1. It Shortens Life: The more frequently one feels angry, disturbed, or disappointed, the fewer days one will have left to live.

2. It Creates Unpleasant Future: If one repeatedly complains and is dissatisfied with circumstances, in the future one is likely to meet with more of the things he/she is upset with. The more people moan the more things they will find to complain about.

3. It damages others: The bad moods and impacts those around you. One should never make others feel terrible since by doing so one is contributing not only to his/her suffering but to the sadness of others likewise.

4. It Causes Negative Effects: Every cause has an effect and therefore one's poor attitude (cause) produces negative conditions. Most people assume it's the other way round, but that's not the case. A person belief determines their circumstances.

Chapter Six

THE DIFFERENCE BETWEEN NEGATIVE ATTITUDE AND BAD MOOD

It's vital to realize that everyone has good days and terrible days. Losing a customer, a terrible presentation or simply having a stressful commute may put a gentle and even-keeled individual in a foul mood.

A poor attitude, however, is often a state of mind, and it can infiltrate a workplace and create a negative atmosphere. As a manager, you may need to choose between adjusting conduct or letting a team member with a poor attitude depart, rather than risk alienating other workers.

What are some examples of workplace attitudes?

Attitude at work may be nice, yet when being addressed it will generally be about a negative attitude. It is vital to distinguish both sorts. It has a huge influence on a company, including productivity levels and morale. So praise excellent attitudes while recognizing weak ones.

There are many examples—essentially, all workplace behavior reflects an attitude of sorts.

Positive attitude at work examples:

- Positive mood
- Mentoring\sIntegrity

Negative attitude at work examples:

- Laziness
- Negative mood
- A 'that'll do attitude
- Aggression
- Blame\sDisruption

From just these brief examples, we're confident you can think of individuals in your business who may fall into either group.

Effects of attitudes on the rest of the team
A cheerful mindset is great—but negativity may be a problem. Some repercussions of negative attitudes conduct toward others include reduced productivity, increased rates of absenteeism, less team cohesiveness, and bad morale.

Negative attitudes impacts

- Lackluster performance
- Unwillingness to cooperate jointly
- Dismal outlook\sUnwillingness to attempt new things
- Reduced energy levels
- Depressive sentiments
- Reduced quality of work product
- Poor customer engagement\sDifficulty overcoming barriers
- Positive attitudes impacts

- Increased productivity
- Greater possibility of cooperation and teamwork\sImproved morale
- Ability to endure adversity
- Willingness to think creatively and attempt new things
- Willingness to exchange information and ideas
- Lower turnover
- Increased feeling of togetherness
- Improved customer service

Chapter Seven

HOW TO GET RID OF BAD ATTITUDE

Studies have demonstrated that how people respond to other persons and situations is mostly determined by their perception and not the real individuals or occurrences.
If you have a bad attitude, you're more likely to adversely affect everything around you. By taking deliberate actions to create optimism, you may counteract and transform a pessimistic mindset.

Method 1 of 2
Letting Go of Negativity

Step 1
Take responsibility for your ideas and actions. You alone are in charge of your life and many of the unpleasant conditions and negative attitudes you carry are affected directly by you. By accepting responsibility for your actions, you may begin to eliminate negativity in your life and build positivity.

Bad ideas generate negative deeds. If you decide to have a good mindset, you'll create favorable changes.

For example, if you are passed over for a promotion at work, it is not because your supervisor doesn't like you and is probably connected to your job performance. Instead of criticizing your employer, speak to him about how you might be better at your work and actively implement these improvements.

Step 2

List bad things in your life and begin to alter them. Acknowledging what is wrong in your life can help you to realize what you can manage and change. Burn the list to signify letting go of negativity.

On a piece of paper, mention everything in your life that you deem bad. Read the list and tick off what you can alter. For example, you may alter unfavorable connections with individuals by eliminating them from your life or you can improve terrible finances by taking efforts to save money.

Once you've thought about ways to alter the bad influences in your life, burn the paper to represent letting go and compose a new list of good things in your life.

Step 3

Let go of expectations. Negativity frequently originates with expectations of yourself or others. Letting up unreasonable or negative expectations will not only help you modify your mindset but will also create a pleasant atmosphere.

Accept that nothing is perfect. Imperfection adds character and letting go of any aspirations of perfection can let you concentrate on the good in any person or circumstance.

Whenever anything awful occurs, ignore it as much as possible and then actively envision things you wish to happen.

Likewise, if a person says anything unpleasant, examine it briefly and then let it go. Dwelling on negativity will just make you feel bad.

Step 4

Forgive yourself and others. Holding grudges and concentrating on your shortcomings will only reinforce a negative attitude. Being able to forgive and let go will help you to concentrate on the good in yourself and others. [4]

The act of forgiving will eliminate bad attitudes and provide room for good ones. But it will also lessen tension and create serenity and quiet in your life.

Step 5

Limit or eliminate negative individuals from your life. The individuals with whom we surround ourselves have a tremendous effect on our attitudes. Limiting or eliminating negative individuals from your life will start helping you modify your mindset.

If you can’t eliminate a person from your life totally, or you don’t want to injure him, you may restrict your exposure to him. You may also offset his negative attitudes and opinions by bringing out the good in what he says or does. This way, you won't be lured down his terrible road.

Step 6\sRespond to change. Negative emotions typically accompany change and the best approach to manage change is to respond and not react to it. Choose to react positively in every scenario and you’ll be able to keep negativity at bay.

You can’t control all events or people, but you can choose how you’ll react to them. Meeting a bad event or person with optimism can keep your mood positive and may also result in a good conclusion to anything.

For example, if someone writes you a harsh email, don't reply to it quickly. Draft a response and wait 24 hours to submit it. Revisit the email the following day and you will likely tone down your reaction, which may prevent a problem from growing.

If something unpleasant occurs, such as losing your job, thank your employer for the chance and remark "this is a chance to find something better that I enjoy."

Step 7
Keep pushing ahead. You'll sometimes have unpleasant thoughts, which are natural and appropriate but learn not to focus on them. By continually going towards the good, you will be able to modify your negative mindset.

Method 2 of 2
Focusing on the Positive

Step 1

See the good in everything. Negative ideas and attitudes are depleting and if you give in to them, they will get stronger. Seeking for the good in any person or scenario can help alter your mentality to a positive one.

Even in the darkest circumstances, there is always something beneficial. It could take some effort to notice, but being able to identify the good elements in everything will help you avoid negativity.
One research demonstrated that a cheerful attitude correlates to achievement more than anything else, including education or abilities.

Step 2

Make a list of everything for which you're thankful. Being appreciative will help create a happy mindset. Listing all of the things for which you’re glad can help you fight any negative thoughts that may occur.

In instances when you feel negative, read the list of things for which you’re thankful. This will remind you to keep optimistic.

Step 3

Use positive language. The language you pick considerably affects your attitude and emotional viewpoint. Using positive phrases and sentiments throughout the day can help you remain cheerful and overcome negativity.

Use statements like "I am optimistic" or "we will find a resolution". These can help you—and everyone around you—stay optimistic

Giving yourself a positive affirmation every morning when you wake up will kick off your day on a good road. For example, you may say to yourself "today is going to be a

terrific day. I feel fantastic and I'm eager to make a difference."
Write encouraging quotations and put them in strategic areas. If you have reminders of great things, you'll be more likely to have pleasant thoughts and sentiments throughout the day.

Step 4\sSurround yourself with positive people. Having helpful individuals around you who can put things in perspective is vital to having a cheerful mindset. Surrounding yourself with positive individuals can counterbalance negativity and help you modify your outlook.

Step 5\sHelp others. Simple acts of kindness and assisting others may do wonders for your mindset. Not only may put things in perspective regarding your life, but it can divert you from troubles and overall make you feel happier.

Consider volunteering at a hospital or soup kitchen. Realizing that you are healthy and have the resources to sustain yourself will put your life in perspective. Doing this might also assist you in actively choosing to change negativity in your life.

Helping friends and family members may also help you shift a poor attitude since you're helping someone else feel good, which in turn will make you feel good.

www.ingramcontent.com/pod-product-compliance
Lightning Source LLC
LaVergne TN
LVHW050011170826
845677LV00023B/3618

* 9 7 9 8 3 5 2 1 4 5 3 4 0 *